C000284379

Permissu superiorum

Nihil obstat

ARTHUR J. SCANLAN, D.D.
Censor

Imprimatur

JOHN CARDINAL FARLEY
Archbishop of New York

Copyright, 1918

THE ENCYCLOPEDIA PRESS, INC.

NEW YORK

Dr. N. P. Leone
gr
7-7-1924

4-21-24 Ⅎ...

PREFACE

This little book has been compiled for beginners who intend to complete a full course of philosophy in two years. In such a course Formal Logic is supposed to be finished by the end of the first three months. This requirement demands not a treatise, but a text-book on Formal Logic, which will comprise the essentials of the subject and serve as a basis for further development and illustration in the hands of an experienced teacher.

Conciseness is one of the chief aims of the book. This characteristic respects the individuality and freedom of the teacher, while for the sake of the student, thoroughness, it is to be hoped, is not sacrificed. Hence controverted points and sometimes examples which the judicious teacher no doubt will suggest are omitted.

The author gratefully acknowledges his indebtedness to the admirable Latin works of J. S. Hickey, O. Cist., and C. Frick, S.J. Some of the examples illustrative of the forms of reasoning have been taken or adapted from the more exhaustive treatise in English of G. H. Joyce, S.J.

Fordham University,
Feast of St. Michael, 29th Sept., 1917.

CONTENTS

Preliminary Notions

Part I

THE FIRST ACT OF THE MIND—SIMPLE APPREHENSION

Chapter I

Chapter II

Chapter III

FINIS

Preliminary Notions

1. PHILOSOPHY. The word "philosophy" means the love or study of wisdom. By "wisdom" the ancients meant the knowledge of all things human and divine which make for right living, as well as the causes by which these things are related or hang together. Hence the aim of philosophy is to answer, in as far as reason is capable of doing so, the last *why* of all things that are. Philosophy is therefore usually defined: *The science of all things from the point of view of their highest or last causes, in so far as this knowledge can be attained by the light of natural reason.*

2. EXPLANATION OF THE DEFINITION—"Science" is a knowledge of a thing through its cause. A cause in its widest sense is that by which a thing *is, becomes,* or *is known.* Philosophy, then, is a science because, like all other sciences, it furnishes us with a systematized body of truths which, resting ultimately on self-evident principles, are united to one another like the links of a chain by an orderly process of demonstration.

"of all things"—Each of the other natural sciences treats of some special department of things, as chemistry, astronomy, medicine, etc., while philosophy takes in a larger field of vision. It embraces the sum total of all things in one complete view.

"highest or last causes"—This characteristic of philosophical knowledge which aims at answering the last *"why"* of all reality differentiates philosophy from

1

all other natural sciences. Other natural sciences furnish the more immediate or proximate, but not the ultimate causes of the objects of their study. Hence philosophy helps to satisfy the yearning of the human mind to explore, as far as it is given to reason to do so, the utmost limits of knowledge.

"by the light of natural reason"—In this way is philosophy marked off from sacred or dogmatic theology. The latter takes its facts and truths from divine revelation. Philosophy depends upon the natural human faculties to acquire its data and to deduce conclusions from them.

3. THE DIVISIONS OF PHILOSOPHY. It is divided into:

LOGIC, which lays down the rules of right reasoning and treats of the means given us by the Author of nature to acquire the knowledge of truth.

METAPHYSICS, again divided into General and Special. The former, called also Ontology, treats of the properties of *Being* in general. The latter applies the notions and principles of Ontology to the primary classes of Substance and investigates their natures and properties. It comprises:

Cosmology, which treats of the nature and origin of the visible world, of the laws to which it is subject and of the nature and constituent elements of bodies in general;

Psychology, which treats of living beings, but principally of the human soul;

Natural Theology, which treats of God in as far as reason enables us to fathom His Divine nature.

MORAL PHILOSOPHY, which discusses the principles of morality and the duties we owe to God and to our fellow men, considered both as individuals and as members of society.

4. EDUCATIONAL AND CULTURAL VALUE OF PHILOSOPHY.

Man has an inborn longing to know the ultimate reasons of things. This longing philosophy in a measure satisfies.

The mental effort which the study of philosophy calls forth imparts, as perhaps no other study does, strength and keenness to the intellectual powers.

It furnishes the mind with a reasoned conviction of the fundamental principles upon which rests all scientific knowledge. It sets forth on reasoned grounds the essential duties of man to his Creator, of the state to its citizens and of the citizens to the state, of man to his fellowmen and to himself.

By the light of sound philosophical principles the divinely authorized teaching of supernatural faith may be more clearly set forth and defended; vital problems of state and private conduct are analyzed and solved; false theories of philosophers and scientists are criticised and refuted; it unifies the conclusions of the particular sciences; it helps to form soundness of judgment; it develops men of thought.

5. ETHICAL VALUE OF PHILOSOPHY.

It is the nature of thought to find its way into action. "The will of man is by his reason swayed" (Shakespeare). Leo XIII says: "It has been implanted in man by nature to follow reason as the guide of his actions, and therefore, if the understanding go wrong in anything, the will easily follows. Hence it comes about that wicked opinions, whose seat is in the understanding, flow into human actions and make them bad. On the other hand, if the mind of man be healthy and strongly grounded in solid and true principles, he will assuredly be a source of great blessings, both as regards the good of individuals and as regards the common weal."

6. THE RELATION BETWEEN PHILOSOPHY AND THE CHRISTIAN RELIGION.

a. Viewed from different stand-points, philosophy is both independent of, and dependent upon, Theology. It is independent: (*a*) by reason of its *object*, namely, "the ultimate causes of all things in as far as they can be known by the light of natural reason". (*b*) By reason of the source from which philosophical knowledge springs—the light of natural reason.

b. Philosophy is dependent upon Theology (*a*) in as far as the light of reason, which belongs to the natural order, ought to be subservient to the light of Revelation, which belongs to the supernatural order. Just as the scientifically demonstrated conclusions of chemistry must be reasonably accepted in physics, or as the acknowledged decisions of our Supreme Court are accepted, in legal matters, by other Courts, so should the acknowledged truths of Revelation be accepted by natural science. (*b*) The guidance of reason which is liable to error, and therefore inferior, ought to submit to the guidance and correction of revealed truth which is absolutely infallible and therefore superior.

"Through the revelation made by the Son of God, a fulness of truth was brought within reach of the human mind of which men had previously no notion. And if it be true, as the ancients had it, that truth is the food of the mind, on which it lives and thrives, the revelation through the Redeemer formed an inexhaustible store from which the human mind might evermore draw new increase of the knowledge which is its life. . . .

"The human mind could adopt either of two attitudes towards revelation. It might accept revelation as truth communicated by God, and make this truth

the criterion and guiding principle of its speculations.
If it did this, revelation became an end to which
natural knowledge was to be subservient. . . .

"Again, the human mind, in virtue of its natural
freedom of election, might abandon the objective
standpoint and fall back upon its own subjective
resources. It might permit its own reason to deal
with revelation in a more unseemly fashion; it might
give reason the first place and revelation the second,
so that instead of reason being subject to revelation,
revelation should be accommodated to the subjective
opinions of the individual; or, on occasion, entirely
denied. This, no doubt, would be a perversion of
right order, but just as man can set himself against the
divinely-established order in the sphere of morals, so
can he set himself in opposition to the divine order in
the sphere of knowledge". (Stöckl—Hist. Phil., Part
II, § 55).

LOGIC

Preliminary Notions

7. LOGIC is either *natural* or *acquired*. The first is that inborn or natural disposition to use one's faculties rightly in the attainment of truth. The second is that same natural disposition cultivated by training. The latter is the subject of the present treatise. It is a necessary study. For untrained reason is liable to err, especially in the solution of more difficult problems.

It may be here noted that any attempt to philosophize at all must presuppose that the human mind can attain truth. The trustworthiness therefore of the human faculties of knowledge must be taken for granted.

That is, they can, by their own nature, attain truth. Otherwise philosophy would be impossible.

8. DEFINITION OF LOGIC. The word λόγος signifies both "thought" and the expression of thought or language—*word*. Thought again necessarily represents some *object*—we cannot think without thinking of something. Logic, then, treats of all three—thought, language and objects. But since in the very nature of things thought comes before language, it follows that Logic treats *primarily* and directly of thought, and *secondarily* and indirectly of language and objects.

Since Logic then has primarily to do with thought or the operations of the rational or intellectual powers of the soul, it is usually defined as:

That art and science which directs the operations of reason in the attainment of truth.

9. EXPLANATION OF THE DEFINITION—
"Art"—An art is a right method or *way* of doing

6

something. The thing which logic sets out to do is to point the way to think aright. And the right way to attain this end is indicated by a system of definite rules. In so far, then, as logic sets forth a collection of rules to direct the mind aright in the way to truth, it is an art. We may distinguish, however, the imparting of the mere knowledge of these rules from the actual use of them. The former is called *Logica docens,* the latter, *Logica utens.* Logic is an art in both senses.

"science"—Science, as we have seen, is the knowledge of things through their causes. In as far as logic, then, gives the reasons or causes why the rules it lays down for right thinking are valid, it is a science.

"which directs"—Sometimes men violate the rules of right thinking and reason ill. Hence to prevent this, certain rules of direction must be known and applied.

"operations of reason"—These operations are ideas, judgments, and reasoning. They form the subject matter (material object) of logic. These same mental operations may be the subject matter (material object) of different sciences. But in that case the stand-point from which these operations are viewed (formal object) will in each case be different for the different sciences. Psychology, for instance, considers these operations from the point of view of their nature and origin; rhetoric with a view of using them for the purpose of persuasion, while it is the province of Logic to direct them as means of attaining truth. To *direct,* then, the operations of reason towards the attainment of truth, is the *formal object* of Logic. Hence we say that the same *material object* may be viewed under different *formalities.*

To ensure that these operations will issue in truth,

two distinct aspects of their truth-giving value must be considered—firstly their conformity to the rules or laws that govern their right procedure as merely *subjective* acts. This secures their *correctness*. By correctness is meant freedom from contradiction and inconsistency. Secondly their conformity to objective reality. It is in this sense they are said to be *true*. Hence it may happen that these operations of reason, or as they are often called intellectual operations, may be *correct* in their procedure without being *true* in their content, and true in their content without being correct in their procedure. From this distinction follows the two-fold

10. DIVISION OF LOGIC—MINOR LOGIC (called also Dialectics and Formal Logic), which has to do directly and primarily with the *correctness* of our thought-operations and secondarily and indirectly with the latter aspect, namely the *truth* of our mental operations;

MAJOR LOGIC (also called Critical and Material Logic), which has to do primarily and directly with the latter aspect, the *truth*, namely, of these same operations, and indirectly and secondarily with their *correctness*.

Many modern authors use the name "Formal Logic" instead of the usual Scholastic term "Minor Logic" and the Aristotelian term "Dialectics". The philosophy of Kant has popularized the term "Formal Logic". But the Kantian concept of this part of Logic is essentially different from the meaning which Scholasticism has assigned to it. In the philosophy of Kant the necessary grooves or laws which the mind must follow in its operations of reason have their origin solely in the mind; they are *of* the mind and *in* the mind.

We must think, Kant would say, according to these necessary laws because our minds, antecedently to all experiences of reality, are constituted that way.

Scholasticism, on the other hand, accounts for these laws of thought, not because our minds are originally furnished by nature with these necessary laws or "forms", but because we discover through experience that reality which is independent of the mind is constituted according to those laws, and that, too, antecedently to our knowing them.

Kant conceives the laws of thought as "forms" native to the mind and therefore as having no objective value. Hence he calls the science of these "forms" "Formal Logic". Scholasticism admits these laws are *in* the mind but not *of* the mind. They are rather engendered in the mind by objective reality. They put us therefore in touch with reality. Hence "Formal Logic" does not mean to Scholasticism what it means to Kantianism.

MINOR LOGIC OR DIALECTICS

11. DEFINITION — Dialectics (διαλέγεσθαι) treats of the processes of reasoning or discursive thought. It may be defined as: *A collection of rules scientifically demonstrated by which the intellect is directed to think correctly.* Hence the subject matter or *material object* of dialectics is the "operations of the intellect or reason"; its *formal object* is "to direct these operations in the way of correct thinking".

12. DIVISION—Since man is by nature characterized by the power of *reasoning*, and since reasoning

involves *judgments* and judgments involve *ideas*, dialectics will treat in turn of each of these mental operations. Again each of these mental processes has its outward expression in language, namely term, proposition, and syllogism. Hence dialectics will treat of "terms", "propositions" and "syllogisms" as the outward signs or expressions respectively of "ideas", "judgments" and "reasoning".

Besides in the pursuit and attainment of truth the human mind, as we shall see later on, naturally proceeds along certain lines, ways or roads. These pathways in the acquisition of truth are explained by what is called Method (μετὰ ὁδὸs).

To sum up then, Minor Logic or Dialectics will treat of:

I.   SIMPLE APPREHENSION OR IDEA AND TERM
II. JUDGMENT AND PROPOSITION
III. REASONING AND THE SYLLOGISM
IV. METHOD

THE FIRST ACT OF THE MIND— SIMPLE APPREHENSION

CHAPTER I

Simple Apprehension and Allied Notions

13. DEFINITION—*Nominal*—Simple apprehension (*apprehendere*) is the act of laying hold of, or grasping something.

Real—The act by which the mind lays hold of an object mentally without affirming or denying anything about it.

EXPLANATION—"The act by which the mind" —Simple apprehension, then, is an *act of the mind*. As such it must necessarily be something within the mind as in its subject. Hence simple apprehension, as an act of the mind, is said to be something *subjective*.

"lays hold on an object". Since it is impossible for the mind "to lay hold or grasp" without laying hold of or grasping something, that *something* is called the OBJECT of simple apprehension. Hence every simple apprehension must necessarily be *objective* as well as *subjective*. When the mind "lays hold of" or apprehends an object, it is said *to know, to perceive, to become aware of an object*.

The object perceived may, of course, have no real existence in nature. It may be only a *possible* object, as when I apprehend "*a golden mountain*". Or again, the manner or mode of the object's existence in nature may be quite different from the mode of its existence as perceived by the mind. For instance I may have a simple apprehension of the object "honesty". I perceive "honesty" in and by itself as if it had a manner or mode of existence in nature by itself, yet "honesty" does not exist in nature independently and by itself, but as the quality inherent in some object.

Lastly the object perceived must be *represented* in some way in the mind; otherwise we could not discern one object from another. Hence every simple apprehension must needs be *representative,* that is, its object must in some way be reproduced in the mind. How this reproduction or representation of the object takes place in the mind is not discussed at present. We only assert the *fact.* Summing up then we arrive at the conclusion that every "simple apprehension" ·must of necessity be:

A. SUBJECTIVE
B. OBJECTIVE
C. REPRESENTATIVE

"mentally". By this word of the definition we guard against confounding *simple apprehension* as an act of the intellect with *sensitive perception* or a sensitive picture in the imagination, which is by philosophers called a phantasm. Imagining is altogether different from conceiving. Sense perception and phantasms men have in common with brutes, while simple apprehension, as an act of the intellect, is the prerogative of man.

The object of sense-perception is always concrete, individual, bound up with matter. It is limited by time, place; it is *here* and *now* and *this,* as this particular triangle (drawn upon the blackboard with yellow chalk). The object of a *simple apprehension*

Koni...

on the contrary is conceived in the mind as abstracted from all limitations of matter—of *nowness, hereness, thisness,* size, color, as a triangle conceived as "a plane figure bounded by three straight lines". It is an object common to many individuals, that is, it is universal. The universal is not picturable.

This distinction is fundamental in all sound systems of philosophy. Failure to recognize this distinction has issued both in the past and present in *Idealism* on the one hand and *Sensism* on the other.

"without affirming or denying, etc.". "Apprehension" for this reason is called "simple", and is distinguished from judgment. A judgment always says something *is* or *is not* something else. Hence an act of judgment always involves two objects of thought, a simple apprehension only one.

Understand well, then, that the simple apprehension is *simple* not because the object apprehended may not be complex, as "the last-rose-of-summer", but precisely because in its character of simple apprehension we do not affirm or deny anything about it, that is, we do not form a judgment about it.

14. **O**THER NAMES F**O**R SIMPLE APPRE-HENSION. Simple Apprehension is also spoken of as an *idea, concept, notion, mental word, mental term.* Each of these words but emphasizes some particular aspect of the same thing. Thus while *simple apprehension* expresses more emphatically the *subjective* and *objective* aspect of the first mental act, *idea* (likeness, picture) lays stress upon its representative value; *concept* (*conceptus*) directs attention to the spiritual generation of the object in the mind. Again, since to apprehend is to know (*noscere*), to take *notice* of an object, hence the result of apprehension is called a *notion* (*notus*). Simple apprehension is called a

mental word, because by it the object is expressed in the mind, and a *mental term* because the simple apprehension may be viewed as a mental *form* or likeness of the object, which *de-term-ines* the mind to know this object rather than that.

It is customary, as it is more convenient in Logic, to speak of *ideas* rather than of simple apprehensions.

15. THE OBJECT OF AN IDEA. That which the idea represents to the mind is called the object of the idea. Objects manifest themselves to us; that is we know them by certain marks. These marks are called "attributes", "qualities", "forms", "determinations", "notes". For instance the paper I write upon is "white", "rectangular", "thin", "made of linen", "smooth". These are called its "notes", etc. We may come to know a greater or less number of these "notes".

THE MATERIAL OBJECT OF AN IDEA—The object itself, viewed as the subject of all its notes, whether we advert to them or not, is called the *material object* of the idea.

THE FORMAL OBJECT OF AN IDEA. That same object, viewed as manifesting to the mind certain notes which we here and now actually come to know, is the *Formal Object* of the idea. The Formal and Material Object are not two really independent objects, but the same object viewed from different points of view.

16. THE COMPREHENSION AND EXTENSION OF AN IDEA. By the *comprehension* of an idea is meant the collection of notes which the idea implies; by the *extension* of an idea is meant the number of individual objects to which the idea applies. It follows then as a general rule that as the comprehension of an idea is *increased*, its extension is

decreased, and *vice versa,* in any series of ideas that have an orderly relation one to the other.

English writers use the term *connotation* for comprehension and *denotation* for extension.

17. OTHER MENTAL P R O C E S S E S IN-VOLVED IN SIMPLE APPREHENSION. That we may the better understand what follows, it is necessary to explain certain mental processes which ideas or simple apprehensions *involve.* They are:

ATTENTION, an act by which the mind directs its powers of thought to one object out of many which lie in its field of vision. To apprehend an object the mind must needs attend to it. Hence every simple apprehension involves an act of attention, whether *voluntary* or *involuntary.*

ABSTRACTION, which is a species of attention. It is an act by which the mind withdraws its attention from all other "notes" which naturally co-exist in an object, and fastens it upon one alone. By *abstraction* the mind does not deny the other notes; it simply *prescinds* from them. For instance we may consider the "color" of a flower to the neglect of the "odor", or we may fasten our attention upon the characteristics of the nature of man—"rational" and "animal" apart from the individualizing notes of this particular man. Since the object of a simple apprehension is *universal,* the mind in conceiving it abstracts from individualizing qualities of that object. Hence an act of simple apprehension involves also an act of ABSTRACTION.

The object in which the "notes" or attributes are found is called the *subject,* and the note or attribute in itself is called a *form,* quality, attribute, etc. (Cf. 15).

REFLECTION, an act by which the mind contemplates its own acts or states. Reflection is two-fold:

Psychological Reflection, when the mind regards its

own acts, or states as facts or modifications of one's own soul;

Ontological Reflection, when the mind regards its own acts or states not precisely as its own, but as representative of objects.

How reflection enters into an act of simple apprehension will appear in the explanation of INTENTION.

INTENTION may be considered *subjectively* as an act of the mind, or *objectively* as an OBJECT upon which the mind's eye is riveted. But when logicians use the word "intention" they usually understand it in an objective sense. It is in this latter sense we shall consider it at present.

Intention is two-fold—first or direct intention and second or reflex intention. It may be observed that a clear knowledge of these terms is essential to the understanding of the Scholastic system of philosophy.

These terms express what experience tells us are the two stages through which the mind passes in the formation of universal ideas. An accurate understanding of their meaning may be difficult for beginners. Yet the light which their study will throw on subsequent logical processes will repay our efforts.

A FIRST or DIRECT INTENTION is an object of our first thought or of our first views of things. I become aware by my sense of sight, for instance, of a "triangle". It will be right-angled, or equilateral, or scalene, or isosceles; it will be drawn with chalk of a certain color; it will be of a certain area; it will be *here, now* and *this.* It will have all the individuating "notes" of a material particular "triangle". At the same instant my intellect spontaneously *abstracts* from this triangle perceived by sense all its individuating peculiarities—its thisness, nowness, hereness, its color, size, etc., leaving before my first direct intellectual gaze only what constitutes a "triangle", namely "a plane figure bounded by three straight lines". This object of thought then, "plane figure, etc.", upon which the mind directly and at first hand rivets its attention, is called a "first or direct intention".

A SECOND or REFLEX INTENTION has for its object something altogether different from that of the *"first intention"*. The object of the *"first or direct intention"* is some reality as it is in itself set out before and independent of the mind. The object of the second or reflex intention is the CONCEPT in the mind of the object of the "first intention". The "first intention" looks out directly upon its object—"the plane figure bounded by three straight lines". The second intention looks back .into the mind for its object, the *concept* namely of "the plane figure, etc.". The second intention therefore is a concept of a concept. Its object is a concept in the mind.

The concept or idea which the mind forms of the object of the "first or direct intention"—the plane figure bounded by three straight lines—is called a "direct universal". It neither includes the individuating notes nor does it explicitly exclude them. It simply neglects them. Considered abstractedly, it is in itself not yet known to be either singular or universal. Yet the notes it represents really exist independently of the mind.

The concept which the mind forms of the concept of the object of the "first intention" is called a *reflex universal,* because the formation of such a concept called for a reflex act of the mind. This reflex universal *positively excludes* all the individualizing notes. Because the mind perceives the Concept within the mind itself in the manner in which it is therein—and the concept is in the mind in a state of abstraction as a result of its first intention. Hence it expresses a certain number of "notes" that are capable of being pluralized in many. The object of thought in the case of the reflex universal embraces both the *object* I conceive (the direct universal) and the *way* I conceive it. Hence the reflex universal is a *logical* or *conceptual entity in the mind*, but with a foundation in reality.

Examples of second intentions are "animal" as a *genus*, "man" as a *species*, "rational" as a *specific difference*.

It is called SECOND Intention because it necessarily presupposes a *First* Intention. It likewise presupposes acts of *reflection*.

ANALYSIS means the act of separating or taking the elements of a thing apart. Analysis of an idea is the act of resolving an idea into its constituent parts whether in its comprehension or extension. The formation of a simple apprehension which results in a universal idea always involves analysis, because the mind by its power of abstraction eliminates individual or accidental characters.

SYNTHESIS is the act of putting things together. Synthesis of ideas means that operation by which the mind unites two or more ideas into one. Thus a composite idea is formed by the union of simple ideas, as when the concept of "man" is formed by uniting the concepts "animal" and "rational".

COMPARISON is the act by which the mind directs its attention now to one idea, now to another, in order to detect the relations between them,—such relations, for instance, as agreement, difference, similarity.

Classification of Ideas

Ideas are classified according to the different stand-points from which you view them. These classifications will help to give your knowledge an orderly arrangement as well as afford an insight into the workings of your own mind. Strive to see these different classes of ideas with the eyes of your mind as clearly as you see bodies with your bodily eyes. This classification we owe to the philosophical studies of centuries. Ideas then may be divided

18. According to their ORIGIN into FACTITIOUS and PRIMITIVE ideas.

A PRIMITIVE idea is one which is formed in the mind by the very presence of its object. If the object is extra-mental the idea of it is said to be *direct*, if the object is intra-mental the idea of it is said to be *reflex*. Primitive ideas are sometimes called *intuitive*.

FACTITIOUS ideas are those which the mind forms by grouping together two or more primitive ideas, or by the analysis of a primitive idea into its elements.

These factitious ideas are either arbitrary or discursive. *Arbitrary* ideas are those that are formed at will or at the bidding of fancy by the union of two or more primitive ideas, as a "golden mountain", or by the analysis of a primitive idea into its elements.

Discursive ideas are those that are the outcome of a reasoning process, as the "idea of God".

Some ideas may be partly primitive and partly fac-

titious, as "a book considered twice as large as it is".
Some factitious ideas may be partly arbitrary and
partly discursive, as "the heroes of fiction".

19. Ideas are also classified ACCORDING TO
THE OBJECTS WHICH THEY REPRESENT.
Now the objects of ideas may be considered either in
their COMPREHENSION or EXTENSION.

A. If we consider their comprehension, ideas are:
SIMPLE and COMPOSITE.

A simple idea is one that contains but one "note",
and does not bear any further analysis, as the idea
of "being".

A composite idea contains two or more "notes" into
which it can be resolved, as "tree", "house".

(Care must be taken to distinguish a "simple idea"
from a "simple being", nor must a "composite idea" be
confounded with a "factitious idea". Find examples.)

CONCRETE and ABSTRACT ideas.

A *concrete* idea expresses a subject *with* a quality
or "form", as "man", "red", "wise".

An *abstract* idea expresses a quality or form *without*
a subject, as "humanity", "redness", "wisdom".

B. If we consider their extension, ideas are:
SINGULAR, UNIVERSAL, PARTICULAR,
COLLECTIVE, TRANSCENDENTAL.

A SINGULAR idea expresses one and only one
individual thing, as "President Wilson", "this man".

(The "notes" that manifest the individual and which
are called "individuating notes" are enumerated by the
ancient logicians in the following verse:

Forma, figura, locus, tempus, stirps, patria, nomen.)

A UNIVERSAL idea expresses one or more "notes"
which can be predicated in the same sense distributively of many. As "man", "American", "white",
"square". By "distributively" is meant that the com-

prehension of the idea can be applied to each of the objects taken separately. The objects to which the universal idea can be applied are called the *inferiors* of the idea.

A PARTICULAR idea is the same as a universal idea but restricted to some *indeterminate* part of its extension, as "some man", "certain poets".

A COLLECTIVE idea is one that is applied to a group of objects taken as a whole, as "army", "family", "flock". It cannot be predicated *distributively* of each individual of the group. An idea that is collective from one point of view may be universal from another point of view, as "army" when applied to the armies of the different nations.

A TRANSCENDENTAL idea expresses that which can be applied not merely to many, but to everything that can be thought of, as "being", "thing", "something", "one", "true", "good". Transcendentals, as we shall afterwards see, are not strictly speaking universals.

VARIOUS KINDS OF UNIVERSAL IDEAS

Since man has the power to judge and reason because his intellect forms universal ideas, it is of paramount importance to understand the different classes of those universal ideas. The brute beasts are incapable of forming universal concepts. Universal ideas are:

DIRECT AND REFLEX.

A DIRECT universal is a nature stripped by the power of abstraction of its individuating "notes" and affirmable of the subject from which it was abstracted, as "man" is affirmed of George Washington. It is the direct universal that is predicated in judgments.

A REFLEX universal is this same nature, "man", for instance, which by an act of reflection upon the way it is conceived in the mind, is now discovered to apply to each and every man. The universal (*universus*) is *one thing* towards which many are *turned* or united, but in such a way that this one thing is found to be multiplied in each of the many. The individuals to which the universal may be applied are called its *inferiors*.

The *direct* is the universal of the "first intention", the *reflex* is the universal of the "second intention". The *direct* is a true universal, because, as a fact, it is a nature found or capable of being found in many, yet before the act of reflection upon the way this nature is conceived by the mind, it is not discovered as something that exists or is capable of existing in many, and therefore not *known* to be a universal.

A. DIVISIONS OF THE REFLEX UNIVERSALS

The logicians have examined the various *ways* in which the things that are common to many are related to their *inferiors*, and they have found, as a result of their inquiry, that those relations fall under five different classes called PREDICABLES, namely, SPECIES, GENUS, SPECIFIC DIFFERENCE, PROPERTY and ACCIDENT. So that whatever it may be that is common to many inferiors, is a species, genus, etc., of these inferiors. But since that which is common to many may be used as a predicate of each, we may define the PREDICABLES *as the various relations in which predicates may stand to their subjects.*

A SPECIES is that which expresses the sum total of the essence of many individuals, as "man". An essence is that which constitutes a thing what it is.

A GENUS is that part of the essence which is common to other species, as "animal".

A SPECIFIC DIFFERENCE is that part of the essence which marks off one species from others of the same genus, as "rational". The genus and specific difference together make up the species.

A PROPERTY is that which, though it does not form part of the essence, yet necessarily flows, from the essence and is always connected with the essence, as the "power of laughter in man".

An ACCIDENT is that which neither forms a part of an essence nor necessarily flows from an essence. It may be present or absent without affecting the essence, as "to walk", "to write poetry".

THE PORPHYRIAN TREE. The various Predicables are well illustrated by the famous Tree of Porphyry.

Substance

Corporeal   Incorporeal

Body

Animate   Inanimate

Living Being

Sensible   Insensible

Animal

Rational   Irrational

Man

John   Peter   James

The HIGHEST GENUS (substance) is that which is not subordinate to any higher genius.

PROXIMATE GENUS is that under which a species is *immediately* contained, as "living being" with respect to "animal", "animal" with respect to "man".

A SUBALTERN GENUS is any genus which is a species of a higher genus, as "living being", "body".

The LOWEST SPECIES (man) is that which has no other species beneath it. All other species above the lowest are called *subaltern species*.

The Porphyrian Tree also illustrates the law of inverse ratio regarding the extension and comprehension of universal ideas in the same field of thought.

B. CLASSIFICATION OF THE DIRECT UNIVERSALS

DIRECT UNIVERSAL IDEAS represent realities. A reality is something not created by the mind, but has some mode of existence independent of the mind, so that the mind by the act of knowing it, simply discovers what was already in existence.

The reflex universal idea is the very same nature or thing as the direct universal, but now clothed with this added characteristic, namely, that which the direct universal idea represents is, or may be multiplied in many individuals. This characteristic *"of one in many"* the mind discovers by an act of *reflection* upon the direct universal idea combined with an act of comparison between what the idea represents and the many inferiors in which it is, or may be found.

Now when we predicate, for instance, that John Smith is an American, we do not mean to say that John Smith possesses the attribute "American" that is common to many; at least we do not ordinarily mean this. We mean rather that John Smith possesses an attribute, "American"—that is a reality, a fact without adverting at all to whether that reality is in John Smith alone or is shared by many others.

Hence what we predicate of a subject is some reality and therefore predicates are represented in the mind by the *direct*, not by the *reflex* universals.

Now we ask the question, what are the highest classes into which all predicates, representative as they are of realities, are divided? We answer with Aristotle that they are divided into ten classes, called CATEGORIES or PREDICAMENTS, namely:

SUBSTANCE, QUALITY, QUANTITY, RELATION, ACTION, PASSION, TIME, PLACE, POSTURE, HABIT.

These are the ten aspects into which all reality is divided. They are the ten highest classes of realities which may be predicated of any subject.

The Categories or Predicaments are therefore *the highest classes into which all reality is divided*.

Take for example an individual named John Smith. You can say or predicate that

John Smith is a rational being (man).. Substance
"   "   " fair-haired .... Quality
"   "   " 5 ft. 10 inches high.... Quantity
"   "   " an American .... Relation
"   "   " working at accounts.... Action
"   "   " fatigued .... Passion
"   "   " (fatigued) at 10 A. M... Time
"   "   " at 42nd Street......... Place
"   "   " seated at a desk........ Posture
"   "   " wearing a negligee shirt. Habit

Any other predicate you may assert of John Smith will be found to fall under one or other of these heads.

A SUBSTANCE is that which exists in itself and does not inhere in another as in its subject, as man, horse, tree.

QUANTITY is the extension of a substance in space.

QUALITY is some determination which characterizes a nature.

RELATION is the order which holds between two things.

PLACE is position in relation to surrounding space.

TIME is position in relation to the course of events.

POSTURE, the relative position of parts in the object itself.

ACTION, the production of change in some other object.

PASSION, the reception of change from some agent.

HABIT is a determination which belongs to the integrity of the subject and equips it for its work. (Cf. Joyce.)

CLASSIFICATION OF IDEAS ACCORDING TO THE PERFECTION WITH WHICH THEY REPRESENT THEIR OBJECTS

20. CLEAR and OBSCURE—

A CLEAR IDEA is one whose notes in kind and number are sufficient to distinguish its object from all other objects.

An idea is OBSCURE when its notes are not sufficient to distinguish its object from others.

CLEAR IDEAS are subdivided into DISTINCT and CONFUSED.

A distinct idea is a clear idea, some notes, at least, of whose object we can distinguished from one another.

A confused idea is a clear idea whose notes we cannot so distinguish from one another.

Distinct ideas are also subdivided into complete and incomplete; *complete* when we can distinguish from one another all the characteristic notes of the object represented, *incomplete* when we cannot.

A COMPREHENSIVE IDEA is one the knowledge of which exhausts all that can be possibly known of its object. Such knowledge is beyond the power of the human mind. Man's knowledge is limited.

A PROPER IDEA is one that is directly derived from its object and thus directly represents its object without any further reference to another object.

An ANALOGOUS IDEA is a proper idea with regard to the objects from which it is directly derived and represents, and applied to other objects because of some resemblance between them and its proper objects. Our concept of God is analogous. We draw from creatures around us ideas that represent Greatness, Power, Wisdom, Truth, Justice, Mercy, Love, Life, Joy, Happiness, etc. Removing from these all bounds we attribute them to God. These attributes in creatures are only faint resemblances to the same attributes in God. But since we cannot see God here face to face, but only as it were imperfectly mirrored in creatures, our concept of Him is only analogous.

An ANALOGOUS IDEA represents its objects partly in the same and partly in different meanings, as the *leg* of an animal and the *leg* of a table. There is a certain resemblance between the *leg* of an animal and the *leg* of a table; they are both *supports,* but there is also a difference, one is the support of an *animate* being, the other of an *inanimate*.

CLASSIFICATION OF IDEAS ARISING FROM A COMPARISON WITH OTHER IDEAS

21. Ideas when compared are COMPATIBLE and REPUGNANT.

COMPATIBLE IDEAS are those which represent

attributes which can co-exist in one and the same object, as "learning" and "prudence" in man.

REPUGNANT IDEAS are those which represent notes that cannot co-exist in the same object, as a *circular* and a *square* figure. Repugnant ideas are called OPPOSITES.

OPPOSITE ideas are those which represent notes that cannot, under the same respect, co-exist in the same thing.

Opposite ideas are divided into four classes—*contradictory, contrary, privative,* and *relative* ideas.

CONTRADICTORY ideas are those that represent any positive attribute or thing and its pure negation, as "man" and "not-man". The opposition between contradictory ideas is called *contradictory opposition*. Contradictory ideas, then, are those of which one sets forth the *negation* of the note or notes which the other asserts. Between contradictories there is no mean. Contradictories not only *exclude* each other, but they both include all things actual and possible. Everything, no matter what it be, whether it be matter or spirit, actual or possible, is either "man" or "not-man". Hence the greatest of all opposition exists between contradictories, because between them there is no medium.

CONTRARY ideas are those which are farthest removed from each other among those which belong to the same genus, as "white" and "black", "sweet" and "sour", "virtue" and "vice". Between contraries there may be a mean or medium. They do not exhaust between them all things. The opposition between contrary ideas is called *contrary opposition*.

PRIVATIVE ideas represent a positive note and its negation or absence in an object in which it is capable of existing or naturally expected to exist, as "sight" and "blindness". You cannot attribute blindness to a stone or a tree, because its opposite, "sight", is not expected to exist in these objects. The opposition between privative ideas is called *privative opposition.*

RELATIVE ideas are those that represent objects, one of which implies that there is another object connected with it, as "parent" and "child", "master" and "servant". The opposition between such ideas is called *relative opposition.*

ASSOCIATED ideas are those which, when one arises in the mind, another is also aroused, as "my college" and my "fellow pupils" or "teachers", etc.

CHAPTER III.

The Outward Expression of Ideas

22. Our ideas would remain hidden in our souls, did we not reveal them by outward "signs". We may make use of many kinds of signs to express our ideas, as gestures, laughter, sighs, etc., but the chief kind of signs we employ is called "Words". "Word" has less extension than "sign". We shall first treat of the meaning and classes of "signs", then the meaning and classes of "words".

SIGNS

DEFINITION—A SIGN is that through which one arrives at the knowledge of something else. Examples—A cloud, smoke, figure of an Indian, etc.

DIVISION of signs—A. By reason of the way the sign signifies something it is either

An OBJECTIVE sign (*Signum ex quo*), a sign which, when previously known, leads to the knowledge of something else, as "rainbow", "the footprints which Robinson Crusoe observed on the sand"; or

A FORMAL sign, i. e. a sign which, though not previously known, leads to the knowledge of something else. It is called also "signum quo". An idea is such a sign. It manifests its object, but it is not itself manifested. Ideas do not as signs previously known represent objects but are forms determining the mind to perceive objects. Knowledge is the reproduction in the mind of objective reality (*cognito est similitudo rei*). The reproduced object in the mind is not the object we know.

30

B. By reason of the connection a sign has with the thing it signifies it is

NATURAL, e. g. Cloud—smoke—idea.

ARBITRARY or Conventional—"three golden balls", "the Stars and Stripes", "words".

WORDS

23. A WORD is an articulate sound uttered by the organs of speech. Words are arbitrary or conventional signs of ideals. They manifest ideas and are substitutes for things. Distinguish carefully between "words" and "signs"; between "words" and "terms".

A TERM in general is the expression of an idea. More precisely a term expresses the whole subject or the whole predicate of a proposition, as "industry-is-a-good-quality-in-a-student"; "a", "good", "in", in this proposition are "words" but not "terms", "industry" is both a "word" and a "term". Hence some words are called *Categorematic*, those namely which of themselves can be used as a term, as "industry". Other words are called *Syncategorematic*, namely those that must enter (syn—with) with one or more categorematic words into the composition of a many-worded term, as articles, prepositions, conjunctions and interjections. What of the verb? The only verb logic recognizes is the verb "is" or "are". The remaining part of other verbs is *logically* represented by a participle or a phrase, as "John loved" would be logically expressed—"John is one who loved". This will be explained more fully under Judgments and Propositions.

TERMS

24. The elements of a *judgment* are two "mental terms", and "the perception of their agreement or dif-

ference"; the elements of a proposition are "two terms" and the "copula". Hence there are

Mental terms—same as Ideas.
Oral   "   —the idea as expressed by speech.
Written   "   —the written expression of ideas.

A *term* (*terminus*) is so called because the subject and predicate terminate or complete a proposition or judgment.

DIVISION OF TERMS

25. We have already set forth the divisions of mental terms or ideas. Generally speaking the divisions of ideas may also be employed as divisions of terms. The following divisions of terms call for special attention:

UNIVOCAL AND EQUIVOCAL terms. An *univocal* term is one that is always employed in the same meaning or comprehension, as "animal" when said of "man" and "brute".

An EQUIVOCAL term is one, which though spelled and pronounced alike, is yet employed in entirely different meanings or comprehensions, as "bit", "box", "chest", "vice". The equivocation is in the word, not in the idea. There is no such thing as an equivocal idea.

ANALOGOUS term. Analogy (ἀναλογία) means comparison or proportion. It is usually defined as a term whose meaning when applied to different objects is partly the same and partly different. We speak, for instance, of the *"food* of the body" and the *"food* of the soul". The meaning of food in both cases agrees in this, that it nourishes and strengthens, in one case the body, in another, the soul, yet it differs inasmuch as the food of the body is different in kind from the food of the soul.

Analogy is *intrinsic* and *extrinsic*.

INTRINSIC analogy is had when that which the analogous term expresses is found within or is intrinsic to the different objects to which it is applied, as "wisdom" when applied to "man" and to "God". Wisdom is found *in* man and *in* God, though in different grades of perfection. In man "wisdom" is finite and dependent, in God infinite and independent.

EXTRINSIC analogy is had when that which the analogous term expresses is *in* or intrinsic to one object and applied to others on account of some relation which the latter objects bear to the former, as "healthy" when applied to animal bodies, to food, climate, color, literature. "Healthy" is said *properly* and *primarily* of an "animal body", because it is a quality *in* or intrinsic to an animal. But "healthy" is applied to food not because it is a quality primarily and properly of food, but because food *causes* health in an animal. "Health" as an effect of food is therefore something outside or extrinsic to the food. The grounds of extrinsic analogy are relations of cause and effect, similarity, resemblance, the relation of the container and the contained, as in the use of "healthy" when applied to food (cause), "laughing" when applied to water (similarity or resemblance to laughter, which properly belongs to the human countenance), "sweet" cup, (the sweetness of the liquid *contained* is transferred to the cup which contains it).

SUPPOSITION OF TERMS

26. The *supposition* or *use* of a term (*supponere*, to stand for) signifies the meaning which is attached to it in a given case.

A term may have a COLLECTIVE or DISTRIBU-

TIVE use. *Collective,* when the term applies to a
number of individuals taken as a group; *Distributive,*
when the term applies to many individuals taken singly
or separately, as "the citizens of New York built the
Brooklyn bridge" (collective) "the citizens of New
York elected a Democratic mayor" (distributive).

REAL AND LOGICAL use. *Real,* when the term
expresses an object as it is in itself, that is, independently of the mind, as "St. Paul"; *Logical,* when it
expresses a mode of existence which is found only in
the mind, as "man" considered as a species. All the
objects of "Second Intentions" are *logical* in their
supposition.

MATERIAL SUPPOSITION or use is had when
the term is used to express itself as a spoken sound
or a sign, as "Cicero is a word of three syllables";
"rattle" is a word whose sound expresses its sense,
The supposition then of a term is nothing else but
the *meaning* which the mind attributes to a certain
term in any particular case.

PART II

THE SECOND ACT OF THE MIND—JUDGMENT

CHAPTER I

Nature of Judgment

27. A Judgment is an act by which the mind perceives the agreement or disagreement between two *objective* ideas, or with St. Thomas, "an act of the intellect whereby the mind combines or separates two terms [meaning two objective mental terms] by affirmation or negation".

EXPLANATION: "An act of the mind" expresses the "genus" of which judgment is a species, just as "animal"—in the definition of man—expresses the "genus" of which man is a species.

"By which it perceives the agreement or disagreement of two objective ideas" is the "specific difference" which distinguishes *judgment* from *"simple apprehension"*.

Because judgment is an "act of the mind", it is therefore not three separate acts of the mind corresponding to subject, copula, and predicate, but one, single act.

"Of two *objective* ideas"—The word "objective" is added to the definition because when the mind says, for instance, that "heat expands iron", the meaning is not, that the mere *subjective* act by which the mind knows heat agrees with the subjective act by which the mind knows "expands iron", but the meaning is that there is an *objective* agreement between "heat" and "a thing that expands iron", that is, that something outside the mind is really so, as a fact.

The essence of the judgment consists in one single flash of perception unitihg or separating two objective ideas.

The two objective ideas are the "matter" of the judgment, that is, that out of which the judgment is made. The "form" of the judgment or that which determines the "matter" to be a judgment and nothing else, is the perception of agreement or difference between the ideas. A judgment therefore is "formally" one simple act, though "materially" a composite act.

What *expresses* orally the matter? The subject and predicate terms. What is the expression of the "form" of a judgment? The words "is" or "is not", "am" or "am not", "art" or "art not", "are" and "are not".

What, therefore, are the prerequisites of a judgment (that is, what is needed beforehand in order that a judgment may be formed)? (1) Two objective ideas; (2) A comparison of these same ideas; (3) Then follows the act of judgment properly, so called, namely, the *perception* of the agreement or disagreement between these two objective ideas.

What is the oral expression of a judgment called? *Proposition.* A proposition, therefore, is a group of words that express a judgment. And, just as two objective ideas, an act of comparison between them and the perception of their agreement or disagreement are the *elements* of a judgment, so the subject-term, the predicate-term and the verbally expressed copula are the *elements* of a proposition.

The copula is in some judgments expressed explicitly, as "Socrates is a man", in others the copula is only implicitly expressed, as "Socrates writes", which, in strictly logical form, is "Socrates-is-writing".

DIVISIONS OF JUDGMENTS

There are certain divisions which have reference to Judgments proper—that is, to Judgments as *"acts of the mind"*. Afterwards we shall give the divisions that are common to both Judgments and Propositions.

DIVISIONS OF JUDGMENT PROPER

28. IMMEDIATE AND MEDIATE: An IM-MEDIATE judgment is one in which the agreement or disagreement of the subject and predicate is perceived without a middle term, or by the mere comparison of both, as "The whole is greater than its part"—"The sun shines".

A MEDIATE judgment is one in which the agreement or disagreement of the subject and predicate is known by comparison of both with a middle term, as the "Three angles of a triangle are equal to two right angles". Briefly an "immediate judgment" is one that is formed without a process of reasoning; a "mediate", through a process of reasoning.

TRUE AND FALSE: TRUE, one that is in harmony with reality: "God exists"; FALSE, one that is not so, "a circle is not round".

UNCERTAIN is one that expresses a doubt or an opinion; CERTAIN is one that is uttered *without* any fear of error, as "Twice two are four"; an "opinion", if uttered with *fear of error*, as "Tomorrow will be rainy".

PRUDENT and RASH: PRUDENT, which rests on serious, RASH, on trivial motives—Consult your experience for examples.

A SYNTHETIC judgment is one, in which the agreement or disagreement of subject and predicate is known by experience alone—as "water extinguishes fire"; "fire burns".

AN ANALYTIC judgment is one, in which either the predicate is contained in the comprehension of the subject, or the subject in the comprehension of the predicate, as (1) "A square has four sides" (2) "A triangle is a figure having its interior angles equal to two right angles".

PROPOSITION

29. A PROPOSITION is the oral or written expression of a judgment. A judgment is an internal act of the mind; a proposition is its external *Sign*.

    a) What therefore are the *elements* of a proposition? Define each. (27)

    b) What constitutes the *matter*, what *the form* of a proposition? (27)

The copula in the logical proposition is always in the *present* tense and in the *indicative* mood.

"Present tense", because though a judgment may be made *about* either *past* or *future* matter, yet that judgment is always made *at* the present moment. The expression therefore that corresponds to that present act of the mind must be in the present tense.

"Indicative mood"—because if not in the *indicative* mood the copula would not express either truth or falsehood. And it is the purpose of Logic to direct the mind *in the attainment of truth*.

It follows therefore that any other tense but the present, and any other mood but the indicative, belong to the *predicate* of the proposition, not to the copula. To reduce any proposition of other tenses and moods to a strictly logical form, change the verb to the appropriate form of the verb "to be" and express its moods or tenses *with the predicate* by other words. For example the logical form of the Proposition "He was my friend" is "He-is-one-who-was-my-friend"; of "Peter will sin" is "Peter-is-a-future-sinner".

In like manner a proposition of one word or two, as "Rain", or "It rains" or "He lives" may be expressed logically "Rain-is-falling", "Raining-is-a-fact", "He-is-living". We have colloquial expressions worded in this logical form, as "He is a-has-been", "He is a goner". The copula does not express the real or actual *existence* or *non-existence* of. the terms, but merely the *identity* or *non-identity* of the terms. Predication therefore is the affirmation or negation of *identity* between two objects of thought.

Exercise. Express in logical form the following: "John broke the window", "The sun may shine to-morrow", "John had seen me in New York yesterday", etc.

Notice that in literary language the subject is not always first,—as "Blessed are the meek", "Great is Diana of the Ephesians".

DIVISIONS OF PROPOSITIONS

30. We may divide propositions according to two main principles—First, on account of something common to all Propositions, namely their essential elements; secondly, by reason of something special to only a certain class of Propositions, namely the *properties peculiar* to this limited class.

If we divide propositions by reason of something common to all, namely their essential elements, we may consider them

A. By reason of the relation between Subject and Predicate or their *Matter*, or

B. By Reason of the extension of the subject, or their *Quantity*, or

C. By reason of the nature of the Copula, or their *Quality*.

A. By reason of the relation between Subject and Predicate Propositions are:

    a. NECESSARY, when the predicate is necessarily related to the subject, that is, when the predicate is such that it springs from the essence of the subject, as "A circle is round".

    b. IMPOSSIBLE, if the predicate is repugnant to the subject, as "an angel is a man".

    c. CONTINGENT, when the predicate is actually in the subject but may not be, as "John is a scholar".

    d. POSSIBLE, when the predicate is able to be, but actually is not in the subject—"The Philippines may be independent".

Laws—All affirmative necessary propositions are true.

    All negative necessary propositions are false.

    All affirmative impossible propositions are false.

    All negative impossible propositions are true.

    All universal contingent propositions are for the most part false.

    All particular contingent propositions are true.

B. By reason of quantity.

The QUANTITY (*quantum*) of a proposition refers to the number of individuals to which the proposition refers. Hence the quantity of a proposition is determined or known by the extension of its subject.

Now the extension of the subject may be—

A. SINGULAR.
B. PARTICULAR.
C. UNIVERSAL.
D. INDEFINITE.

So propositions are divided by reason of their extension or *quantity* into:

A. Singular, whose subject is a singular term, as "Peter is a Saint".

B. Particular, whose subject is a particular term, as "Some men are learned".

C. Universal, whose subject is a universal term, as "All men are mortal".

D. Indefinite, whose subject is not determined by any sign of its extension, "Soldiers are greedy for glory".

We have seen that a proposition is singular, universal, particular or indefinite, when its subject is singular, etc. The quantity of a proposition, therefore, depends upon the extension of its *Subject*.

Now a Universal Proposition may be Universal in three ways. It may be:

Metaphysically
Physically } Universal
Morally

A proposition is METAPHYSICALLY universal when it is such that it holds in all cases, so that no exception is possible even by the power of God, as "The whole is greater than any of its parts", "Man is a rational animal". These propositions are also called "absolute", "necessary", "a priori", "analytical".

A PHYSICALLY Universal proposition is one which admits no exception in the order of nature, but may admit of an exception in the supernatural order, that is, through the power of God working a miracle, as "Fire burns". Propositions of this kind are also called Contingent, Hypothetical, a Posteriori, Synthetic.

A MORALLY Universal proposition is one which is ordinarily true, yet may, with difficulty, have exceptions, as "Mothers love their children".

C. By reason of their FORM (copula), propositions are affirmative or negative: *Affirmative* when the identity of the subject and predicate is affirmed; *Negative* when the identity of the subject and predicate is denied.

Keep well in mind that in a negative proposition the negative "not" must be bound up with the copula, that is, form one piece with it. Should the negative be added, not to the copula, but to the predicate, the proposition would be affirmative, as "Man-is-not-a-brute", whereas, "Man-is not-a brute" is negative. Hence, "Rebellion-is-not to acknowledge the authority of lawful government" is an affirmative proposition. In the same way, if the negative affects the subject, but not the copula, the proposition is affirmative, as "He who does not gather with me scattereth". The negative particle need not necessarily stand between the subject and predicate, thus "No bird is a quadruped" is negative. It is sufficient that the negative may be construed with the copula.

Hence mark you well, the Extension of the subject of a Proposition is referred to as its *Quantity;* the Form of a proposition, that is, its standing as affirmative or negative, is referred to as its *Quality.*

Laws That Regard the Extension of the Predicate

31. The predicate of an affirmative proposition is always a *Particular term,* as "A horse is an animal" means not that "horse" can be applied to all and each inferior under the term "animal", but a horse can be applied to some only of the inferiors of animal. There are two important cases where this law is not true. One of these exceptional cases will appear in the chapter on Definition, another in Ontology.

The predicate of a negative proposition is always a *Universal Term,* as "A man is not a tree", or "No man is a tree", the meaning is that "Man is not this or that or any other tree". Hence tree is denied of man *Universally.*

Another way of expressing these laws is: "The *Predicate* of an affirmative proposition is *not distributed or taken Universally;* while the predicate of a negative proposition is always distributed or taken Universally".

These laws are of the utmost importance, as you shall afterwards see. Considering both the quantity and quality of propositions, logicians have called for brevity's sake:

UNIVERSAL affirmative propositions—
A Propositions.

UNIVERSAL negative propositions—
E Propositions.

PARTICULAR affirmative propositions—
I Propositions.

PARTICULAR negative propositions—
O Propositions.

For the future, then, we shall use for brevity's sake, the letters A, E, I, O, instead of universal affirmative, etc.

The laws or rules for the distribution of the two terms in a Judgment or proposition may be thus briefly expressed. In A only the subject is always distributed; in E both the subject and predicate are always distributed; in I, neither the subject or predicate is distributed; in O, only the predicate is distributed.

Reflect upon these rules, until they become perfectly familiar to you.

OTHER DIVISIONS OF PROPOSITIONS

32. Propositions are: Simple, Complex or Compound.

A SIMPLE proposition is one which affirms or denies one predicate of one subject, as "God is charity", "Man is not a brute".

A COMPLEX proposition is a simple proposition that has a complex term for the subject or predicate. By a complex term is understood a many-worded term that expresses not merely the nature of a thing denoted, but also one or more qualifications belonging to it, as "The tall man with a cane whom I met on the road very early this morning is blind on account of an accident that had befallen him ten years ago". Remember, though a term may be grammatically complex, it still forms only *one single* logical term. For the logician it is *simple*.

A COMPOUND proposition is one in which are joined together many simple propositions, as "A pious man does good and avoids evil". "Hearts, tongues, figures, scribes, bards, poets cannot speak, write, sing numbers of his love for Anthony".

Now, compound propositions are divided into two classes: EXPLICIT (*aperte compositi*), those whose compound character is *apparent* from their grammatical construction, as the example above; IMPLICIT (*occulte compositi*), those whose grammatical structure does not *manifest* or make apparent their composite nature. These in English are called "Exponibles", as "God alone is eternal".

EXPLICIT COMPOUND Propositions are: COPULATIVE "Life and death depend upon God". "Neither riches nor honors make one happy".

ADVERSATIVE, when the parts are connected by the particles "but", "nevertheless", etc.: "The heavens and earth shall pass away *but* the word of God shall never pass away". "It is necessary that scandals come, *nevertheless* woe", etc.

RELATIVE, when the parts are connected by "as—so", "where—there". "As you sow so shall you reap"; "Where charity abounds, there will happiness be".

CAUSAL, when parts are connected by "for", "because", "since", etc. "Blessed are the meek, for (because) (since) they shall possess the land".

CONDITIONAL OR HYPOTHETICAL, when introduced by "if".

DISJUNCTIVE, when introduced by "either—or". Now, since there is really only one assertion in conditional and disjunctive propositions we may class them with *simple*.

IMPLICIT COMPOUND Propositions are:

EXCLUSIVE, as "God *alone* is eternal"; i. e., "God is eternal and no other being is eternal".

EXCEPTIVE, as "All but one perished"; i. e., "One did not perish, and all others did". Exclusive and exceptive are practically the same.

COMPARATIVE, as "Obedience is better than sacrifice"; "Sacrifice is good, but obedience is better".

REDUPLICATIVE, as "A man, inasmuch as he is an animal, feels". To perceive the full force of an "exponible" proposition, *all that it implicitly implies ought to be explicitly stated.*

Chapter III

Modal Propositions

83. A MODAL proposition is one which asserts not only that the predicate is or is not in the subject, but also the *way, mode,* or *manner* in which the predicate is or is not in the subject, as "God is necessarily just". Modal are opposed to pure propositions.

Whenever the copula is qualified by such words as *necessarily, possibly,* or by *must, may, can, cannot,* the *proposition is modal.*

There are four kinds of ways or modes by which the subject may be connected with the predicate. Hence modal propositions are:

NECESSARY
CONTINGENT
POSSIBLE
IMPOSSIBLE

Modal propositions may be reduced to simple propositions, thus:

S must be P=S is necessarily P or, that S is P is a necessity.

S cannot be P=That S be P is an impossibility.

S may be P=That S be P is a possibility, etc.

CHAPTER IV

Relative Properties of Propositions

84. We have already spoken of such properties as belong to propositions whether you think of other propositions or not, such as quality and quantity, etc. Hence they are called *absolute* properties. *Relative properties* belong to propositions when compared with one another. There are three kinds of properties which belong to propositions when compared one with another: *opposition*, *æquipollence* or equivalence (*æquipollentia*), and *conversion*.

OPPOSITION

OPPOSITE propositions are in a wide sense those that have the same subject and predicate and differ in quantity or quality or in both.

Opposition is in a more restricted sense the affirmation and negation of the same predicate regarding the same subject at the same time and under the same respect.

What then are the three requisite conditions in order that propositions be opposed?

There are four species of opposition:

    (a) Contradictory (b) Contrary.
    (c) Sub-contrary (d) Sub-altern.

CONTRADICTORY PROPOSITIONS are those which, having the same subject and predicate, differ both in *quantity* and *quality*.

CONTRARY PROPOSITIONS are those which, having the same subject and predicate, differ in *quality* alone.

SUB-CONTRARY PROPOSITIONS are two particular propositions which, having the same subject and predicate, differ in *quality*.

SUB-ALTERN PROPOSITIONS are those which, having the same subject and predicate, differ in *quantity* alone.   The following diagram explains at a glance the different kinds of opposition.

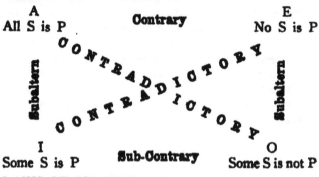

A
All S is P   **Contrary**   E
No S is P

I   **Sub-Contrary**   O
Some S is P   Some S is not P

LAWS OF OPPOSITION:

(a) Contradictories cannot be at the same time true, nor at the same time false.

(b) Contraries cannot be at the same time true, but they may be at the same time false.

(c) Sub-contraries may be at the same time true, but cannot be at the same time false.

(d) Sub-alterns can be at the same time true and at the same time false.

Prove each of these laws.

ÆQUIPOLLENCE or EQUIVALENCE or OBVERSION

1. Definition:

ÆQUIPOLLENCE is the reduction of two opposite propositions to the same signification by the use of the negative particle.

Thus—

    S a P All men are mortal=No men are
            not-mortal.   S e $\overline{P}$

    S o P No philosophers are practical=All
            philosophers are not-practical. S a $\overline{P}$

    S i P Some j u d g e s are just=Some
            judges are not not-just.   S o $\overline{P}$

    S o P Some ministers are not wise=Some

Rule.   ministers are not-wise.   S i $\overline{P}$

Change the quality of the proposition and substitute
for the predicate its contradictory term.

THE CONVERSION OF PROPOSITIONS

35. The conversion of propositions means the changing of subject into the predicate and predicate into the
subject without changing the meaning.

Conversion is either:

    a. SIMPLE, when the *quantity* is preserved.

    b. ACCIDENTAL, when the *quantity* is not
       preserved.

    c. By CONTRAPOSITION we mean the con-
       version that is applicable to O and A. To
       obtain the contrapositive, first equipollate
       or obvert and then convert the proposition.

Rule for the Conversion of propositions:

Simpliciter fEcI convertitur; EvA per acci.

AstO per contra; sit fit conversio tota.

The original proposition is called the "Convertend";
the proposition that results from Conversion, the
"Converse".

PART III

THIRD ACT OF THE MIND OR INTELLECT—REASONING

Chapter I

Nature of the Act of Reasoning

36. Just as in the case of simple apprehension and term, judgment and proposition, so also we may consider the act of the mind in reasoning and the expression of that act. Like judgment, reasoning is an act by which the mind perceives the agreement or disagreement between two objective ideas, but it differs from judgment in this, that in reasoning the mind perceives the agreement or disagreement between two ideas *through the medium* of a third idea, whereas in a judgment proper the mind perceives the agreement or the disagreement between two ideas *without the aid* of a third idea.

In other words Judgment in the ordinary sense is an act of *immediate* perception; Reasoning is an act of *mediate* perception of the agreement or difference between two ideas.

Every act of reasoning, therefore, is a judgment, though *mediate;* but every judgment is not an act of reasoning, because a judgment may be *immediate.*

PREREQUISITES OF THE ACT OF REASONING—Just as the act of immediate judgment had its prerequisites (recall them) so also has the act of reasoning its prerequisites, namely:

51

a. Three ideas.
b. The comparison of two of the ideas with the third.
c. The perception of the agreement or disagreement between these two ideas and the third idea, in other words the formation of two judgments.
d. Lastly, the perception of the agreement or disagreement of the two ideas, thus compared with the third, between themselves. This is precisely and *formally* the act of reasoning.

We may therefore define the act of reasoning thus: *"Reasoning is that act of the mind* (intellect) *by which the agreement or disagreement of two ideas is perceived through a comparison between them and a third idea"*.

QUESTION—What, therefore, is the *remote* matter of reasoning; what is the proximate matter; what is the form of reasoning?

The laws of thought on which the act of reasoning rests are:

a. The law of IDENTITY or AGREEMENT. *Things that are identical with the same thing are identical with one another.* This principle is self-evident and cannot itself be proved. It needs no proof. This is the principle on which rests every *affirmative* conclusion in reasoning.

b. The law of DISAGREEMENT or DIFFER-ENCE. *Two things, one of which agrees with a third thing, and the other of which disagrees with the same third thing, disagree with each other.* This is also self-evident, and needs no proof, nor can it be proved. It is the principle on which rest all *negative* conclusions in reasoning.

Both these principles may be reduced to one, namely, to the *principle* of *Contradiction,* which is stated thus: *"The same thing cannot be affirmed and denied of the same thing at the same time, and under the same respect".*

CHAPTER II

The Expression of the Act of Reasoning

37. The sign or the expression of the Act of Reasoning is called an argumentation or Syllogism (thinking together). It is defined thus: *A syllogism or argumentation is an inference by which, from two propositions a new proposition is derived, the truth of which follows from these two as a necessary consequence.*

TECHNICAL TERMS INVOLVED IN A SYLLOGISM

First regarding the terms contained in the syllogism
  - a. There are three terms: Minor, Major, Middle.
  - b. The Minor term is the S; the Major, the P of the Conclusion.
  - c. The Middle term is the term employed *as a means* or medium of comparison between the Minor and Major.
  - d. The Middle term is repeated twice.
  - e. These three terms constitute the *Remote* Matter of the syllogism.

Secondly, regarding the propositions of the Syllogism
  - a. There are three propositions.
  - b. The first two are called the *premises*, the last is called the *conclusion*. One premise is the Major, the other premise the Minor.
  - c. The Major premise contains the Major term. It gives the relation between the Major and Middle terms.

d. The Minor premise contains the Minor term.
It gives the relation between the Minor
and Middle terms.

e. The Major and Minor premises taken together are called the *antecedent*. The conclusion is called the *consequent*.

f. The truth of the conclusion is therefore
conditional because the truth of the conclusion of a syllogism depends upon the
truth of both premises.

g. The Consequence (*consequentia*) is the connection in thought (*nexus*) between the
Major and Minor premises. Its sign or
expression is "therefore".

h. The three propositions are the proximate
"matter" of the syllogism. The "form" is
the connection between bot'..

Note—The "form" is the same as the "Consequence".

The number of terms is not to be judged by the
number of words. Many words can *form
one term*.

The syllogism is said TO BE IN FORM, when
the premises are properly arranged for the
purpose of drawing the conclusion.

The conclusion is said to be "*virtually*" contained in the premises, that is, the conclusion does not actually exist in the
premises, but the premises have the power
of producing it. The premises are also
said to contain the conclusion *implicitly*
but not *explicitly*.

We are now treating of what is called the
Categorical Syllogism, that is, one that is
made up of categorical propositions. A

categorical proposition is one that affirms or denies *absolutely* the agreement or disagreement of the subject and predicate. It is opposed to Conditional or Hypothetical Syllogisms and also to Disjunctive Syllogisms.

Chapter III

Rules of the Syllogism

38—1. There must be three and only three terms: the Major, Middle and Minor.

2. No term must be distributed in the conclusion, which is not distributed in the premises.

3. The Middle term must never be found in the conclusion.

4. The Middle term must be distributed in one, at least, of the premises.

5. Two affirmative premises can never give a negative conclusion.

6. No conclusion can be drawn when both premises are negative.

7. If one of the premises is particular the conclusion must be particular; and if one of the premises is negative, the conclusion must be negative.

8. From two particular premises no conclusion follows.

NOTE: Of these rules No. 1 and No. 3 refer to the structure of the syllogism; No. 2 and No. 4 refer to its quantity; No. 5 and No. 6 refer to its quality; No. 7 refers to quantity and quality.

PROOF OF THE RULES

39. Rule 1. From the nature of the act of reasoning the syllogism must have three terms, because when we cannot perceive the agreement or disagreement between two terms, we must have recourse to a third as a means (medium) of comparison. We cannot have four terms, because then there could be no comparison.

To secure three and only three terms, each term must be univocal. If any term is equivocal or ambiguous then there are really more than three terms. Examples of syllogism with equivocal terms:

All chests are boxes,	Man is a species,
A part of me is a chest,	Socrates is a man,
∴ A part of me is a box,	∴ Socrates is a species.

In both Syllogisms is the fallacy called *"Ambiguous Middle"*.

Rule 2. Should the conclusion be wider than the premises, then there are really four terms—three in the premises, while the excess of extension found in the conclusion amounts to a fourth term—and this excess in the extension of the conclusion was not compared in the premises with the Middle term.

Examples:

All "Pierce-Arrows" are automobiles.

A "Ford" is not a "Pierce-Arrow".

∴ A "Ford" is not an automobile.

This fallacy is called the "Illicit process of the Major" or the "Illicit process of the Minor".

Rule 3. First, because the office of the Middle term is to serve as a means of comparing the Minor and Major of the conclusion. Hence it does not belong to the conclusion.

Secondly, the conclusion contains the result of the comparison between the Minor and Major. That result therefore has to do with the Minor and Major, not Middle. The Middle is the means of arriving at the result, not the result itself. Therefore it is outside that result, and hence has no place in the conclusion.

Examples:

Cicero is an orator.

Cicero is a Roman.

∴ Cicero is a Roman orator.

Rule 4. Unless the Middle term is distributed at least once you may have four terms. Because if the Middle term is taken particularly twice, one of the extremes may be compared with the Middle term in one part of the latter's extension and the other extreme with another and different part of the extension of the Middle term.

Examples:

All crocodiles are animals.

All men are animals.

∴ All men are crocodiles.

All queens are women.

All female cooks are women.

∴ All female cooks are queens.

This fallacy is called—"Undistributed Middle".

Rule 5. It is impossible for two terms (Minor and Major) to agree with the third (Middle) and disagree between themselves. Yet a negative conclusion would demand such an impossibility.

Example:

All birds lay eggs.

The ostrich is a bird.

∴ The ostrich does not lay eggs.—This conclusion is absurd.

Rule 6. Because, when both premises are negative, it is impossible to have any comparison between the extremes (Minor and Major) and the Middle term. For the extremes cannot be *connected* with the Middle in any one of the premises.

Example:

Philosophers are not elephants.

Socrates is not an elephant.

∴ Socrates is not a philosopher.

Rule 7. If one or other of the premises is negative,

the conclusion must be negative. For when one extreme is identical with the Middle term, and the other extreme disagrees with the Middle term then the extremes must disagree with each other. This disagreement can be expressed in the conclusion only by a negative proposition.

If both premises are affirmative and one is particular, they both distribute but one term between them. This distributed term must be the Middle term. But the Middle term cannot be in the conclusion. Therefore there is nothing left for the conclusion but two undistributed terms. And a conclusion with two undistributed terms must be a particular.

Rule 8. If both premises are particular affirmative, no term in these premises can be distributed.

If one premise is affirmative and the other negative, they both have only one distributed term. But since the conclusion must be negative (Rule 7) two distributed terms would be needed in the premises. Therefore, since there are not two, nothing can follow.

CHAPTER IV

Moods and Figures of the Syllogism

40. MOOD—Definition. A "Mood" is the arrangement of the premises by reason of their quality and quantity.

The propositions that make up the premises of every categorical syllogism are the typical propositional forms, A, E, I, O. Since there are but two premises, and each of these must be one of the four propositions A, E, I, O, it follows that there are but sixteen possible arrangements of premises, thus:

AA	EA	IA	OA
AE	EE	IE	OE
AI	EI	II	OI
AO	EO	IO	OO

All these combinations cannot be employed as premises of a syllogism. If we examine each of these combinations under the light of the Rules of the Syllogism, some will be found to be illegitmate. Thus:

    a. EE, EO, OE, OO have two negative premises, and must be rejected by Rule *Six*.

    b. II, IO, OI, OO have two particular premises, and must be rejected by Rule *Eight*.

    c. IE—This involves an illicit process of the Major term. For the conclusion must be negative (Rule *Seven*).. The predicate of this negative conclusion must be *distributed*. This necessitates that the Major term should be distributed in its premise. But it is not. For I does not distribute any of its terms. Therefore a conclusion

> drawn from IE must be vitiated by an
> illicit process of the Major. Therefore
> the mood IE must be rejected. A valid
> conclusion may be inferred from IE, but
> such an inference would not be drawn in
> the ordinary way.

The possible moods therefore are *eight* in number, one combination of EI, and seven combinations which contain the premise A.

FIGURES

41. We must now examine which of these combinations or "moods" may be employed in the several Figures.

FIGURES OF THE SYLLOGISM—Definition: A "Figure" is a form of the syllogism, determined by the position of the Middle term in the two premises. There are only four possible positions, hence four figures. They are:

Figure 1.	Figure 2.	Figure 3.	Figure 4.
M. P.	P. M.	M. P.	P. M.
S. M.	S. M.	M. S.	M. S.
——	——	——	——
S. P.	S. P.	S. P.	S. P.

There are special rules for each figure:

Fig. 1) a. The Minor premises must be affirmative.
      b. The Major premises must be universal.

Fig. 2) a. One premise must be negative.
      b. The Major premise must be universal.

Fig. 3) a. The Minor premise must be affirmative.
      b. The conclusion must be particular.

Fig. 4) a. If the Major is affirmative, the Minor must be universal.
      b. If the Minor is affirmative, the conclusion must be particular.

c. If the conclusion is negative, the Major
    must be universal.

In the light of these rules of the figures, you can
discover the "moods" that are valid for each figure.
These "moods" will be found to be nineteen. They
are enumerated in the following mnemonic lines:

Barbara, Celarent, Darii, Ferioque, *prioris.*
Cesare, Camestres, Festino, Baroco, *secundae.*
Tertia, Darapti, Disamis, Datisi, Felapton,
Bocardo, Ferison, *habet; Quarta insuper addit.*
Bramantip, Camenes, Dimaris, Fesapo, Fre-
    sison.

The reason why we have only a certain number and
certain kinds of moods in each figure:

Figure I.

Rule 1. Excludes AE, AO. Rule 2. Excludes IA,
OA. Therefore four remain available for the First
Figure:

AA EA AI EI.

Hence the mnemonics "Barbara, etc".

Figure II.

In this figure Rule 1, excludes AA AI IA.
    Rule 2, excludes IA OA.

Hence the available moods are EA AE EI AO.
Hence "Cesare, etc.".

Figure III.

Hence the valid moods in this are AA IA AI EA
    OA EI.

Hence "Darapti, etc.".

Figure IV.

There are five valid moods, AA AE IA EA EE.
Hence "Bramantip, etc.".

CHAPTER V

Reduction

42. Aristotle held that only in the first figure is the validity of our conclusion absolutely evident. The first figure is perfect; the others, though valid, imperfect. The moods in the other figures are *manifestly* conclusive when they are reduced to the form of the first figure.

REDUCTION is defined as the process by which a syllogism in one of the other figures is expressed as a syllogism of the first.

Now the names of the various moods, as given in the mnemonic lines are so ingeniously constructed as (1) to indicate the moods of the first figure, to which the moods of the other figures may be reduced; and (2) what logical operations are necessary to achieve the result.

(1) Every mood begins with one of the letters B, C, D, F. These letters indicate respectively the mood of the first figure to which each is to be reduced. Thus "Cesare" to "Celarent, etc.".

(2) Of the consonants composing the body of each word, the letters s, p, m, c are employed. These letters tell us what logical changes are required to obtain a syllogism in one of the moods of the First Figure. s)=(*simpliciter* — simple conversion). It means that the premises indicated by the preceding vowel must be converted "simply".

p)=(*per accidens*). That the premise preceding it must be converted "per accidens".

m)=(*muta*, change). That the premises are to be transposed.

c)=(contradictory proposition). Indicates that the reduction is to be *indirect* or "per impossible".

Now proceed to the operation of Reduction.

The process which gives us a syllogism in the first figure precisely equivalent to the original syllogism is termed *Direct or Ostensive Reduction.* This kind of reduction presents no great difficulty.

There are, however, two moods, Baroco Figure 2, and Bocardo Figure 3, to which the Direct or Ostensive Reduction cannot be applied. To reduce these moods the *Indirect* Method of Reduction must be applied.

This consists in admitting by way of hypothesis that the conclusion of the mood may be false, and in showing, by a syllogism in Barbara that this supposition involves the falsity of one of the original propositions. The original propositions are, however, known to be true. Hence we are forced to admit the conclusion in Bocardo and Baroco valid.

Take the following Syllogism in Baroco:

All whales are aquatic animals.

Some mammals are not aquatic animals.

∴ Some mammals are not whales.

If the conclusion is false the contradictory must be true "All mammals are whales".

We now use this proposition and one of the original premises to form a syllogism in Barbara—thus:

All whales are aquatic animals.

But all mammals are whales.

∴ All mammals are aquatic animals.

Now this conclusion is the *Contradictory* of one of the original premises: "Some mammals are not aquatic animals". This last by supposition is true. Therefore the conclusion arrived at in the second syllogism is false. But the error does not lie in the reasoning, for this is the first figure. The error must lie, therefore, in the fact that one of the premises of the last syllogism is false. The premise "all whales are aquatic animals" is, however, given as true. Therefore the error crept in by supposing "all mammals are whales" to be true. It is therefore false and the contradictory must be true—the original conclusion of Baroco.

This "Indirect" Method of Reduction may be applied to any Mood, in place of the Ostensive Method.

CHAPTER VI

Hypothetical Syllogisms

43. A HYPOTHETICAL SYLLOGISM is one whose Major premise is a hypothetical, and whose Minor is a categorical proposition. The Major furnishes the ground for the inference, while the Minor states a case in which the Major is applicable.

LAW GOVERNING THE HYPOTHETICAL SYLLOGISM. The truth of the consequent follows from the truth of the antecedent, and the falsehood of the antecedent follows from the falsehood of the consequent.

Rules of the Hypothetical Syllogism,—Only two (1) To posit the antecedent is to posit the consequent, and (2) to sublate the consequent is to sublate the antecedent.

Hence only two moods.

(1) The Constructive—as, If A. is B., C. is D.
But A. is B.
∴. C. is D.

(2) The Destructive —as, If A. is B., C. is D.
But C. is not D.
∴. A. is not B.

Hence there are two *fallacies* to which these syllogisms are liable, namely

(1) The fallacy of denying the antecedent.

(2) The fallacy of affirming the consequent.

Examples:

(1) If icebergs are approaching our Atlantic seaboard we shall have cold weather.

But icebergs are not approaching our Atlantic seaboard.

∴. We shall not have cold weather.

This conclusion does not follow.

(2) If Samuel's real estate depreciates in value he will be bankrupt.

But he will be bankrupt.

∴ Samuel's real estate depreciates in value.

This conclusion does not follow.

Of course you can have a purely hypothetical syllogism, that is, one in which the major and minor premises as well as the conclusion are hypothetical propositions, as

If C. is D., E. is F.
If A. is B., C. is D.
∴ If A. is B., E. is F.

Attempts have been made to reduce Hypothetical Syllogisms to a Categorical form, but such a process would not be a Reduction properly so called.

CHAPTER VII

The Disjunctive Syllogism

44. Definition. A DISJUNCTIVE SYLLOGISM is one in which the major premise is a disjunctive proposition, and the minor a categorical proposition, either affirming or denying one or more members of the opposition.

It has two moods.

    1. Modus ponendo tollens, as
        S is either P or Q.
        But S is P.
        ∴ S is not Q.

    2. Modus tollendo ponens, as
        S is either P or Q.
        But S is not P.
        ∴ S is Q.

RULES: (1) To affirm one or more alternatives is to deny the remaining alternatives. (2) To deny one or more alternatives is to affirm the remaining alternatives.

FALLACIES: (1) Care should be taken that the disjunctive should exhaust all the alternatives of the case, in other words that the disjunctive should be complete. For example:

John is either in the Law or Medical department of Fordham University.

But he is not in the Law department.

∴ He is in the Medical department. He may be in the Collegiate department.

(2) The alternatives should be mutually exclusive. For example:

John is either in Fordham University, or in the Collegiate, Law or Medical department.

But John is in Fordham University.

∴ John is not in the Collegiate, Law or Medical department. This conclusion does not follow.

Criticise the following arguments:

John is either sleeping or not sleeping.

But John is sleeping.

∴ John is not sleeping.

John cannot walk and be seated at the same time.

But John is not at present seated.

∴ John is walking.

CHAPTER VIII

Abridged and Conjoined Syllogisms

45. Fully expressed syllogisms are rare in conversation, in oratory, in argumentative literature. What is usual in practice is the use of imperfectly stated syllogisms, either simple or complex.

SIMPLE ABRIDGED SYLLOGISMS

The *Enthymeme*—(ἐν-θυμός) is a form of argument in which the major or the minor or the conclusion is not expressed. One of the premises or the conclusion is suppressed or kept in the mind.

> *Examples:* Major premise omitted—
> "He is a coward for he is a liar".

> Minor premise omitted—
> "He is a coward for all liars are cowards".

An enthymeme need not be categorical. It may also be pure hypothetical or pure disjunctive or any mixture of these various forms. Examples: "If crime is rampant the police of the city is not good; for daring and reckless criminals are always in the minority".

> "Were he a child of Adam, he would do the works of Adam; which he does not".

> "Our vicious propensities are such that we must either fall into sin and misery or practice self-denial".

The enthymeme may easily become a cover for a fallacy. Certain principles not universally true, others not scientifically proved are adopted by certain classes of people as if they were really universal and acknowledged by all scientists as true, and these certain classes who hold these principles reject any statement as false which may contradict their spurious principles.

Examples:

"He is a Catholic, therefore he is not a good American citizen".

"He is poor, therefore he is degraded".

"He cannot read or write, therefore he cannot make a good citizen".

"He is a student of Richdale, etc., therefore he is a refined gentleman".

"He is an Englishman, therefore he is a noble character".

"He is a Jesuit, therefore he is a sly intriguer".

"He is Irish, therefore he is not worth much".

"Catholics do not admit complete evolution, therefore they are wrong".

"He belongs to the Hebrew race, therefore he must be persecuted".

"He is a Catholic, therefore he is intolerant".

"Divorce is an assertion of freedom, therefore it is right".

REASONING BASED on principles generally but not universally true is subject to the same fallacy—such as "tramps are not to be trusted".

Epicheireme—An argument to one or both of whose premises is an annexed reason to support it, as:

Whatever is spiritual is immortal; for it is incapable of corruption.

But the human soul is spiritual.

∴ The human soul is immortal.

This form of reasoning is commonly used by orators. It may be drawn out into an ordinary syllogism, as:

Whatever is incapable of corruption is immortal

But whatever is spiritual is incapable of corruption.

∴ Whatever is spiritual is immortal.

But the human soul is spiritual.

∴ The human soul is immortal.

Sorites—An argument in the first figure with many Middle terms.　It is based on the principle of the "dictum de omni", as:

Socrates is a man.

All men are mammals.

All mammals are animals.

All animals are living creatures.

All living creatures are substances.

∴ Socrates is a substance.

This form of argument may be expressed in as many syllogisms as there are middle terms in the sorites.

THE DILEMMA

46. The *Dilemma* (the horned syllogism) whose Major is a disjunctive proposition containing two members, about each of which something contrary to our adversary is proved.

Hence it is plain what Trilemma and Quadrilemma are.

There are four kinds of dilemmas:

A. Simple constructive, where there are two or more antecedents in the Major premise, and one consequent. In the constructive dilemma, the Minor is an *affirmative* disjunctive.

Example: If I go out, I catch a cold; if I stay in, I catch a cold.

But I either go out, or stay in.

∴ I catch a cold.

B. Complex constructive where there are several antecedents and several consequents.　The Minor is again an *affirmative* conjunctive.

Example: If education is popular, compulsion is
unnecessary.

If unpopular, compulsion will not be
tolerated.

But education is either popular or unpopular.

∴ Either compulsion is unnecessary or
will not be tolerated.

C. Destructive—where there are several antecedents
in Major, and a negative disjunctive in the Minor.

Example: If this man were wise, he would not abuse
the Bible in jest; if he were good, he
would not do so in earnest; but either
he does it in jest or in earnest.

∴ He is not wise or not good.

The dilemma is of great value to the orator.

Rules: (1) The enumeration of the alternatives
should be complete and mutually exclusive.

(2) See to it that your dilemma cannot be retorted
by your adversary. A dilemma is retorted by showing
that whichever alternative is chosen the conclusion
opposite to yours may logically follow.

(3) A dilemma may hide many fallacies. In order
to detect them, reduce the dilemma to syllogistic form.

CHAPTER IX

Induction

47. So far we have been dealing with *deductive* reasoning. In brief, deduction is a reasoning from the universal, to a less universal, to the particular, or to the individual, from what is true, of "all" to what is true of "some", or one. Its starting point is a general principle.

In order, then, to reason deductively at all, it is plain that the mind must previously have arrived at the knowledge of universal truths, judgments, or propositions.

The important question to be now answered is: *How do we arrive at the knowledge of universal truths, judgments or propositions?*

Before answering this question let us recall that every universal judgment is either *immediately* or *mediately* ANALYTIC or SYNTHETIC.

IMMEDIATE ANALYTIC UNIVERSAL JUDGMENTS. Examples of such judgments are: "The whole is greater than any of its parts"; "Everything that happens must have a cause". A little reflection will enable us to discover that we arrive at the knowledge of immediate analytic universal judgments, not by a process of reason, but by the immediate mental processes of (1) observation, (2) abstraction, (3) generalization, by which we reach the universal concept of their subjects and predicates, between which, by the processes of comparison and analysis, the mind *intuitively* perceives a necessary connection. Take the judgment: "The whole is greater than any of its parts".

In the first place, by a simple act of *observation*, we come to know, let us say, this individual whole orange, and this individual part of it.

By *abstraction* we may neglect the individuating notes of "this orange" and "this part of it", and by generalization, form the universal concepts—"whole" and "part", which may apply to any "whole" and "part".

Then we compare and analyse the concepts "whole" and "part" of any object. The outcome of this comparative analysis will be an immediate, intuitive, universal and necessary judgment—"The whole (every whole) is greater than any of its parts". The necessary connection of the subject and predicate is based upon the simple comparative analysis of the nature of "whole" and "greater than any part". This process of forming immediate, universal, analytic judgments may be called, in a *wide sense*, Induction.

MEDIATE ANALYTIC JUDGMENTS are arrived at by the process of deductive reasoning, as when it is demonstrated that "The sum of the three angles of a triangle is equal to two right angles". Pure mathematical conclusions are the outcome of mediate analytical judgments.

IMMEDIATE SYNTHETIC JUDGMENTS are those of which the agreement or disagreement of the subject and predicate is warranted, not by a comparative analysis of their subjects and predicates, but by an observed fact of experience. For example: "Some shrubs are thorny". There is nothing in the universal notion of "shrub" and "thorny" to compel the mind to affirm this judgment. The affirmative connection between "shrub" and "thorny" rests for its justification upon an observed sense-fact of experience.

MEDIATE SYNTHETIC UNIVERSAL JUDG-

MENTS. It is observed, for example, that a five-dollar gold piece and a feather placed in the exhausted receiver of an air-pump, fall through equal vertical spaces in equal time. Other materials are experimented with in the same way. The same result follows. Then it is concluded that "All bodies fall through equal vertical spaces in equal times". This is mediate synthetic universal judgment.

At first sight it looks as if this conclusion is not justified. How is it possible to reach such a conclusion about *all* bodies, though we have experimented only on *some?* How is the mind justified in bridging the chasm between "*some*" and "*all*"? This leap moreover seems to violate the rule of reasoning that "the conclusion cannot have a greater extension than the premises". We can clearly see the validity of the conclusion about the "some" on which we have actually experimented, but how are we justified in predicating of "all" what we know by experience of "some" only?

Other examples: Science tells us that "All diamonds are combustible", though on very few has the experiment been performed. "All potassium floats in water"; "H and O combine to form water". In fact, scientists admit that we may from one observed case arrive at a universal law. How this can be is the problem of scientific *Induction*.

SCIENTIFIC INDUCTION—In general it is a process by which from comparatively few observed cases, we discover laws that govern the activities or phenomena of the material world.

Scientific Induction comprises the following steps:

A. OBSERVATION—Certain facts of phenomena presented to the senses are observed. These facts may become known either by observation of events in the course of *Natural Occurrences*, or by observation of what happens as the result of *artificially arranged experiments*. Take an example from the events of common life. Several persons at the same banquet were temporarily poisoned. This is an observed fact. It serves as a starting point for the investigation of its cause by the Inductive process. Observation of facts is the first step in an Inductive reasoning.

B. HYPOTHESIS—The question is, then, naturally asked: How did the fact of poisoning happen? What was its cause? The human mind naturally seeks the cause of observed phenomena. The investigator examines the menu, and finds that among the dishes served at the banquet was lobster. He suspects the lobster may have been tainted. So among the antecedents of the poisoning he hits upon tainted lobster as the cause of that phenomenon. So far the cause selected is only a supposition, a tentative explanation, a clever guess. It may or it may not be the true cause. Such a supposed cause is called a hypothesis.

A hypothesis, then, is a supposed cause of a phenomenon provisionally selected with a view of eventually ascertaining the true cause of the phenomenon in question. Since a hypothesis is only a supposed cause, it would be irrational to accept it as the real and certain cause of the phenomenon which it professes to explain.

Hypothesis is so called because the form of reasoning in the case expressed by a hypothetical or conditional syllogism thus: "If the guests ate tainted lobster, then poisoning would follow. But poisoning did follow". From this syllogism we cannot conclude "Therefore the guests ate tainted lobster", because some other unsuspected cause may have produced the poisoning. At best the only conclusion we may validly draw is—"tainted lobster *may possibly* be the cause".

Beware, therefore, of accepting a mere hypothesis, as popular scientific books and magazine articles too often do, as a final and certain scientific conclusion.

A hypothesis to be admissible must be

    a. Possible.

    b. It must explain all the main facts of experience in the case.

    c. It must not either in itself or in its consequences contradict any other certainty, known fact or law.

C. VERIFICATION—Verification, the third step in an Induction, is that process by which the investigator tests whether the supposed cause (hypothesis) is the real, true cause of the phenomenon under consideration. In the example chosen, verification endeavors to confirm whether the real cause of the phenomenon — poisoning — was tainted lobster. The author of the hypothesis will continue his investigations to discover whether some other unknown agency might not have played a part in causing the poisoning. (a) He will endeavor to eliminate every possible intruder. (b) He will draw conclusions by *deduction* from his hypothesis and observe whether these conclusions agree in other cases, with the facts of nature. (c) He will continue his investigations until he is convinced that the supposed cause is the only necessitating cause of the phenomenon. When he is satisfied that the tainted lobster alone produced the poisoning, then he concludes that the former was the true cause of the latter. VERIFICATION IS THE KERNEL of the whole process of Induction.

D. GENERALIZATION—The process of generalization is based upon the rational assumption that constant phenomena must have their sufficient reason in the *fixed* nature of an active cause, in this case, of tainted lobster, which will always act in the same way. This constant way of action inherent in the nature of causal agencies is called THE LAW OF THE UNIFORMITY OF NATURE. And this uniform tendency of natural agencies to act in the same way is not of itself a self-evident principle, like the law of causation, but finds its ultimate explanation in the will of an all-wise and omnipotent Ruler of the universe.

Induction, then, rests on a few important principles which it must assume to justify its conclusions, (1) the principle namely of causality (analytic—self-evident) and (2) the principle of the uniformity of nature, which may be thus stated: *Physical non-free causes, when they act in similar circumstances, always and everywhere produce similar results.*

Induction is usually divided into COMPLETE and INCOMPLETE Induction:

COMPLETE Induction is the process by which we predicate of a whole class of things what we have already predicated from experimental reasons, of each individual in the class.   Example:

John, James, Henry, etc., passed successfully their examination in philosophy.

John, James, Henry, etc, make up the entire class. Therefore the entire class passed successfully the examination in philosophy.

INCOMPLETE INDUCTION or Scientific Induction is the process by which we rise to a universal law from our experience of a limited number of cases. It draws a conclusion about "all" from our experience of "some".   It is an inference from particular to general, from what comes within experience to what is beyond experience.

WHAT IS THE RATIONAL EXPLANATION OF THIS MENTAL PROCESS FROM THE PAR-

TICULAR TO THE GENERAL? It certainly needs justification. This justification cannot rationally rest upon experience itself. Experience at best extends to only a few cases. Hence Empirical and Positivist Philosophy, which teach that all knowledge is confined to experience, *that the world outside experience is unknowable,* utterly fail to justify their own pet form of reasoning, Induction.

According to Scholastic philosophy the ultimate justification of the *law of the uniformity of nature* rests on the will of an all-wise Creator, Who has endowed physical agencies by His free will with regular, constant modes of activity.

Incomplete Induction is so called not because it cannot issue in certain cases in complete certainty, but because all the possible cases are not, nor need they be, experimented upon.

METHODS OF SCIENTIFIC INDUCTION

THE METHOD OF AGREEMENT. When a phenomenon has occurred in several different cases, and these different cases have a single circumstance in common, this common circumstance is *probably* the sufficient reason or cause of the phenomenon. Briefly "the sole invariable antecedent of a phenomenon is probably its cause". Example—Suppose several persons had eaten lobster at the same meal and were prostrated by ptomaine poisoning, the lobster was probably the cause of their sickness.

METHOD OF DIFFERENCE. "Whatever is present in a case when the phenomenon to be investigated occurs, and absent in another when that phenomenon does not occur, other circumstances remaining the same, is the cause or partial cause of that phenomenon". Example—A bell is rung in a jar containing air. The sound is heard. The air is removed. The bell is again struck. The sound is not heard. We conclude that the air is the transmitting cause of the sound.

THE METHOD OF REMAINDERS OR RESIDUES. "When the part known to result from certain antecedents, already determined by previous inductions, is eliminated from the phenomenon, that which is left of the phenomenon is caused by the remaining antecedents". Example—My lamp has been lighted two hours. The temperature of my room has risen from 65 degrees to 70 degrees. How explain the additional 5 degrees? The increase of heat is due to the lamp and my body. There is no fire. The lamp is now burned for the same length of time while the room is unoccupied. The temperature shows an increase of 4 degrees. I conclude that my body was the cause of the additional 1 degree.

THE METHOD OF CONCOMITANT VARIATIONS. "When the degrees of variation of a phenomenon correspond with the degrees of variation of the antecedent, it is to be presumed that there is between the two a relation of causality, immediate or mediate". Example—Instead of striking a bell in a complete vacuum we can strike it with very little air in the receiver of the air-pump. We then hear a faint sound, which increases or decreases every time we increase or diminish the density of the air. This shows that the air is the cause of the transmission of sound.

CHAPTER X

Analogy

48. An argument from analogy (ἀναλογια —proportion) is one that is based upon an equality of proportion between two acts or instances. There is for example a certain equality of proportion between the law of gravitation and the heavenly bodies on the one hand and submission to lawful authority and the citizens of a state on the other hand, which may be stated in mathematical form thus:

Heavenly bodies: gravitation: citizens: authority. Hence we may argue that as

The heavenly bodies submit to the law of gravitation

Therefore the citizens of a State ought to submit to the lawful authority.

The principle underlying an argument derived from an equality of proportion is: What can be predicated of one pair of related terms may be also predicated of the other pair of related terms. The conclusion is valid when the argument is based upon those points in which the relations are exactly the same, but invalid when based upon points in which the relations are different. There exists, for instance, to a certain extent,.an equality of proportion between

Individuals: state: members: human body.

There are, it is true, relations between individuals and the State which in certain points are exactly the same as the relations between the members and the human body. Yet individuals have other relations, with God for example, which make the relations of the individual to the State different from the relations

of the members to the body. To argue, therefore,
that just as the members are entirely subservient to
the body so individuals are entirely subservient to the
State, would be invalid.

There are, in addition to this kind of argument based
on an *analogy of proportion*, arguments based on an
analogy of general *resemblance*. If one instance re-
sembles another in important respects, we argue that
what is predicable of the first instance may be predicable of the second. Thus:

The Earth and Mars are alike in several respects—
both are planets, both revolve round the sun, both turn
on their axes, both have an atmosphere and change of
seasons.

But the earth is inhabited.

Therefore Mars is inhabited.

This argument is not reliable because there may be
many important points of difference between the two
planets. And the validity of the inference in such
cases will depend upon the points of resemblances when
compared with the points of difference.

An argument from *example* is also based on resemblances, but is more often employed to stimulate
action rather than impart knowledge. Even when the
purpose is knowledge, example is used rather *to illus-
trate* what is already known than to discover what is
yet unknown.

CHAPTER XI

Fallacies

49. A FALLACY or sophism is an argument in which a falsehood is hidden under the appearance of truth.

Divisions—1. Fallacies arising from the "language" (*fallaciæ in dictione*). 2. Fallacies arising from the matter (*fallaciæ in re*).

I. Fallacies in Language are:

Equivocation—arising from the employment of the same word in different senses.

Amphibology—arising from the doubtful or ambiguous meaning of the grammatical construction.

Composition—when that which is true only of things taken separately is understood of them taken together.

Division—when that which is true only of things taken together is understood of them taken separately.

Accent—arising from the difference of stress laid on a particular syllable of word.

Figure of Speech—when we mistake the meaning of one word with that of another whose form is similar.

II. Fallacies in matter:

Accident—where predicates that essentially belong to the subject are confounded with those that accidentally belong to it.

A dicto secundum quid ad dictum simpliciter, and vice versa.

Refuting the wrong point (*Ignoratio Elenchi*)—"barking up the wrong tree".

Begging the question—*Petitio principii*—Vicious Circle.

Consequent—The fallacy of the Hypothetical Syllogism.

False cause—*non causa pro causa; post hoc, ergo propter hoc.*

Many questions.

False induction—

    a. *Ab uno disce omnes.*

    b. False observation.

    c. Confounding a hypothesis with a scientific certainty.

    d. Seeing what we wish to see.

    e. Not seeing what we do not wish to see.

    f. False interpretation.

Examples of each of these fallacies are given in the course of the class lectures.

CHAPTER XII

Definition

50. DEFINITION is the expression in words of the *nature* of a thing. Definition then belongs to the Logic of the simple apprehension. It declares the essential characteristics of a thing. It has to do with Comprehension. It presents a *distinct* idea of the subject and the essential characteristics stand in the predicate. It is this predicate that is the definition.

KINDS OF DEFINITION. Definition is either real or nominal. NOMINAL DEFINITION is one that declares the *meaning* of the word. It has to do with the word, that is its sense or meaning in as far as the word is the *name* (*nomen*) of a thing. This quasi-definition is usually expressed by giving the derivation of the *word* defined, as "infinite" means "without limit" from "in" not, and "finis", a limit.

A REAL DEFINITION is one which explains the nature of a thing. And it explains this nature by giving the characteristics of the thing. Real definition may be

GENETIC (genesis—origin), which gives the process by which the thing is produced, as: A circle *is a figure that is formed by the evolution of a line in a plane around one of its extremities.* It does not give its essential characteristics, nor its properties, but simply tells how it has come to be.

DESCRIPTIVE DEFINITION is one, which gives such a combination of properties, accidental features, circumstances, etc., as suffice to make the object recognizable. It is the literary definition. It does not enter into the essence of the object.

ESSENTIAL DEFINITION is one which is formed by the "genus" and "specific difference" of a thing. This is the strictly philosophical definition. It gives the species of the thing, because the species of a thing is made up of the "genus" and "specific difference", as "man is a rational animal". The "essential definition" is rarely attained.

Now we can give the essential definition of but few objects. We know a lion is different from a horse, but we cannot penetrate the essential difference between them. In most cases we must be content with definitions by properties.

RULES OF DEFINITION. (1) The definition must be clearer than the thing defined. (2) The definition must not be negative unless in case of negative or privitive ideas. (3) The definition must be adequate, i. e., the subject and predicate must have exactly the same extension. (4) The definition must not contain the thing defined. (5) The definition must not contain metaphors. (6) It must be concise. Experience teaches that examples, which for the sake of making an impression on the memory may have a local coloring, are best given by the teacher in the course of the lectures.

CHAPTER XIII

Division

51. DIVISION is the complete and orderly separation of a unit or whole into its constituent parts.

A unit or whole (*totum*) is some one thing which contains in itself several things into which it can be split up. These several things contained in a "whole" are called its "parts".

There are several kinds of "units" or "wholes", which we must carefully distinguish. There is:

A. The REAL unit or whole which exists in the real order of things. It has, therefore, real parts—"Man", for instance, is a real unit or whole, because "man" exists in the objective order of things independently of our mind. We can distinguish in "man" as a real unit or whole different kinds of parts:

PHYSICAL PARTS, those namely that can be actually separated. For example "body" and "soul" are physical parts of "man". Since body and soul are essential to "man", they are called ESSENTIAL PHYSICAL PARTS.

Other physical parts may be distinguished in man and likewise can be actually separated. But these parts, though they contribute to the entirety or integrity of a man, are yet not absolutely necessary or essential to man, as leg, arm, etc. A man remains a man though he may lose an arm or leg. These are called INTEGRAL PHYSICAL PARTS.

Again we can consider those parts in man
which, though they cannot be really separated one from another in "man" like the
essential physical parts and the *integral
physical parts*, yet may be *mentally sep-
arable*, that is by different concepts of the
mind.

For instance, the "animal nature" and the "rational
nature" in man. They can be separated, not actually
or physically, but only in thought. Such parts are
called *metaphysical parts*, and "man", considered as
made up of such parts, is a "metaphysical whole or
unit".

B. There yet remains another kind of "whole" or
"unit", and consequently other kinds of parts, namely,
a *logical or potential unit or whole* and *logical or
potential parts*".

A logical or potential whole or unit is a universal
idea". It is called "logical" because, though it represents what actually exists (direct universal) yet its
object does not exist in the way it is conceived in
thought, λογος, because it is conceived by the mind
abstracted from all individuating notes.

It is called "potential" because it is *capable* of being
predicated of many "inferiors", myriads of which do
not exist and perhaps never will exist. For the extension of a universal idea covers not only the individuals
which now actually exist, or have existed, but also all
those that may possibly be, because to all of them the
object represented by the universal idea applies.

RULES OF DIVISION—

(1) A division must have one and only one basis or
principle of division.

(2) It must be adequate or complete.

(3) The constituent parts must be mutually exclusive.

(4) Each step of the division must be proximate.

(5) It must, if possible, be positive.

The aim of definition is to make *clear* our ideas; the aim of division is to make *distinct* our ideas.

PART IV

METHOD

CHAPTER I

Synthetic and Analytic Method

52. Method (*μετά ὁδός*) means a *way* or *road towards*. When applied to logic it means a way or road which is most advantageous to follow in the attainment, exposition and defense of truth, or scientific knowledge.

There are two such roads or methods, namely the *Synthetic* and the *Analytic*.

THE SYNTHETIC METHOD. Some sciences set out from a few simple ideas and a few necessary, universal principles; mathematics, for instance, is such a science. The mathematician then proceeds to combine these elementary notions, in order to deduce from them other new, less simple, more complex relations. He proceeds *synthetically* and therefore his method is called synthetic.

The Synthetic Method, then, is that which proceeds from the universal to the less universal and particular. It is also called the *deductive method*. The sciences to which it is applied are called *deductive sciences*. This method predominates in philosophy and theology as well as in mathematics.

THE METHOD OF ANALYSIS. When, on the other hand, a science starts from concrete individual facts which observation and experiment pre-

Lightning Source UK Ltd.
Milton Keynes UK
UKHW021320270123
416064UK00006B/582

9 781017 607109